Where Do I Go from Here?

Patricia Hawthorne

Where Do I Go from Here?

Stepping into the Purpose You Were Created For

Patricia Hawthorne

Pearly Gates Publishing, LLC, Houston, Texas

Where Do I Go from Here?

Where Do I Go from Here?
Stepping into the Purpose You Were Created For

Copyright © 2019
Patricia Hawthorne

All Rights Reserved.
No portion of this publication may be reproduced, stored in any electronic system, or transmitted in any form or by any means (electronic, mechanical, photocopy, recording, or otherwise) without written permission from the publisher. Brief quotations may be used in literary reviews.

Print ISBN 13: 978-1-947445-50-5
Digital ISBN 13: 978-1-947445-55-0
Library of Congress Control Number: 2019933094

Scripture references are taken from the New King James Version, New International Version, King James Version, New Living Translation, and English Standard Version of the Holy Bible and are used with permission from Zondervan via Biblegateway.com. Public Domain.

For information and bulk ordering, contact:
Pearly Gates Publishing, LLC
Angela Edwards, CEO
P.O. Box 62287
Houston, TX 77205
BestSeller@PearlyGatesPublishing.com

ACKNOWLEDGMENTS

First, I want to thank **God** for giving me the strength and courage to write this book.

To **Angela Edwards**, CEO of Pearly Gates Publishing: Thank you for your guidance, patience, and expertise sowed into this project. I appreciate you and am grateful for your God-inspired creativity.

To the many people who inspired and motivated me to continue in the midst of obstacles: Thank you. I also want to thank **Christian Faith Ministries, Dr. Gregg,** and **Dedra Thomas** for waking up the gift of exhortation within me, inspiring me to open my own inspirational greeting card business. I made my own cards and penned words of encouragement to others.

Next, I want to thank my children who were so supportive. My son, **Kevin Estelle**, encouraged me to follow my dreams. My daughter, **Andria Jackson**, inspired me to go to college at the age of 66.

Special thanks to **Les Brown** and all the online coaches who invited me to webinars, emailed me inspirational information and sent motivational videos that helped me to get unstuck and elevated my faith. Although I knew what I

Where Do I Go from Here?

wanted to do, I didn't know how to get started. I truly appreciate all of you staying in contact with me by email year after year.

A heartfelt thanks to all of my family: my husband, **Royal Hawthorne, Sr.**; mother, **Millie Owens**; sisters and brothers, **Cherlyn, Katie, Elouise, Elvira, Bea, Gwen, Shannon, and Lawyer**; and my present church family, **Mt. Zion Baptist Church with Rev. Larry Caldwell, Sr.**, for their constant support and encouragement. My husband worked diligently with me on releasing my new CD. All of my family supported me in every event. My mom is my inspiration and my example of a Virtuous Woman. She is 89 years old and is still teaching Sunday School for over 50 years! She has inspired me to be a woman of excellence and has taught me persistence.

I am richly blessed through all of you. I am immensely grateful to all of you for being there for me. Thank you for helping me to step into the purpose for which I was created.

"The Lord bless you and keep you. The Lord make His face shine upon you, and be gracious to you. The Lord lift up His countenance upon you, and give you peace."
~ **Numbers 6: 24-26, NKJV** ~

INTRODUCTION

Ask yourself these questions:

- ➢ What value lives within me?
- ➢ What do people need from me?
- ➢ How do people change or transform from what I give them?

Hello! Patricia Hawthorne, here. I am so excited to share this good news with you! I bring you seeds of inspiration, encouragement, and hope. You are filled with passion and purpose. So, light your fire and start moving. Persevere and be persistent!

You are called to encourage and influence humanity. My desire is to encourage you to live your dream and fulfill your purpose in life. My goal is to help you see who you really are, inspire you to recognize the value within you and empower you to go forth and reach your full potential. I hope to give you the courage to get back up when you fall and confidence to keep moving when the road gets tough.

Can I tell you a secret? You have unlimited power living inside you, but you have not used it

Where Do I Go from Here?

to its fullest potential. You have greatness and purpose living within you. There are dreams you have yet to turn into reality, talents you have not developed, and purpose you have not fulfilled.

We are all here for a reason. We are all filled with gifts and talents that are waiting to inspire another. Everything we need to move forward and fulfill our purpose is already within us. Discover your awesome purpose and begin moving forward. Walk by faith and not by sight.

If you can believe it, you can receive it!

If you can believe it, you can achieve it!

This is your season to start your business, write "that" book, or put those new ideas into action! Don't delay; don't procrastinate. Ignite your goals today! You may not know how or what to do, but I implore you to pray for wisdom and understanding. Seek out those who will encourage and empower you to move forward. Do what you can and work with what you have. It's truly your season. Arise and fulfill your destiny! Step out on faith and do what you've been called to do!

Do you realize people inspire people? You are called to encourage and influence man, making a difference throughout the land! Remember: **GREATNESS** is living in you! **POWER** is living in you! *PURPOSE* is living in you! You are filled with potential. Go forth today and release all the wonderful gifts within you!

Where Do I Go from Here?

"TRANSFORMED" A POEM BY PATRICIA HAWTHORNE

I am **TRANSFORMED**; I'm brand new.
I want to do all I'm **CALLED** to do.
Called to **ENCOURAGE** and influence man,
Making a difference throughout the land.
Here I am. Here I stand
With my **PURPOSE** in my hand.
With a **PASSION** and desire.
With a heart burning with fire.
With ideas and energy,
I'm inspired for victory.
I'm moving forward day by day
With **PERSISTENCE** leading my way.
I'm moving forward with a made-up mind,
Staying focused all the time.
If I fall…If I fail,
I shall rise to prevail.
No matter what people may say,
I see the **VISION** from far away.
No matter what comes against me,
I have a date with destiny.
I'm pressing on. My goal is near.
I won't **PROCRASTINATE**; I won't fear.
If there's a will, there's a way.
I'm on course, and I won't stray.
I'm **DEDICATED**. I won't give in.
I'm **DETERMINED** to reach the end.

TABLE OF CONTENTS

ACKNOWLEDGMENTS VI
INTRODUCTION VIII
"TRANSFORMED" XI
A POEM BY PATRICIA HAWTHORNE XI
STEP ONE: WHO ARE YOU? 1
   GET YOUR MIND RIGHT 2
   FORGET THE PAST 5
   YOU ARE TRANSFORMED 8
STEP TWO: WHY ARE YOU HERE? 15
   PRAY 16
   CONSIDER YOUR PASSION 19
   DISCOVER YOUR PURPOSE 24
STEP THREE: MOVE FORWARD 31
   SEE THE VISION 32
   PURSUE YOUR PURPOSE 36
   BE PERSISTENT 40
STEP FOUR: NEVER GIVE UP 47
   First: Be Patient 49
   Second: Be Consistent 51
   Third: Be Determined 53

Where Do I Go from Here?

CONCLUSION..56
LIFE-CHANGING STEPS MADE SIMPLE..........57
ABOUT THE AUTHOR...................................59
CONTACT PATRICIA.......................................61

Patricia Hawthorne

> I AM **TRANSFORMED**;
> I'M BRAND NEW.
> I WANT TO DO ALL
> I'M **CALLED** TO DO.
> CALLED TO **ENCOURAGE**
> AND **INFLUENCE** MAN,
> MAKING A DIFFERENCE
> THROUGHOUT THE LAND.

"Be ye transformed by the renewing of your mind."
~ Romans 12:2 ~

STEP ONE

WHO ARE YOU?

Patricia Hawthorne

GET YOUR MIND RIGHT

Philippians 4:8 KJV

*"Finally, brethren, whatsoever things are true, whatsoever things are honest, whatsoever things are just, whatsoever things are pure, whatsoever things are lovely, whatsoever things are of good report; if there be any virtue, and if there be any praise,
think on these things."*

Where Do I Go from Here?

"Think on these things." Let them be the object of your careful attention and study. Practice them. Think about your obligation to observe them. Think about the influence which they may have on those around you. Remember, thoughts produce actions and actions produce results. Keep yourself surrounded with positive thoughts, people, and things that will inspire you.

So, who are you? What value lives within you? What do people need from you? How do people change from what you give them?

Do you know you have great potential? You have a purpose. You have the power to make a difference. You have the power to impact, change, and transform lives.

For a long time, I thought I was here to do what everybody else was doing: work, go to church and take care of my family's needs. I thought that was all there was to life because that's what my parents did—until one day, I realized I was somebody worthy and capable of doing whatever I set my mind to do.

Patricia Hawthorne

I remember as a child growing up, I was always looking for love in all the wrong places because my father had left me when I was just a baby. Deep inside, I longed for fatherly love. While in high school, I became pregnant. I recall the deep shame and persecution I felt. I had no desire to drop out of school; instead, I had every determination to complete my education. So, I decided to go before the school board to request to be able to finish as the first pregnant student.

I received such wonderful favor. I believe I was permitted to stay because I was an 'A' student, had an excellent record, and came from a well-known and respected family. After having my baby during that Summer, I went back to finish school and graduate as the first married student.

Yes, I sometimes regret the poor choices I made, but they have made me stronger and wiser today.

Never look down on a person because you don't know their story. Never voice your negative opinion of another until you walk in their shoes.

FORGET THE PAST

Philippians 3:13 NLT

"No, dear brothers and sisters, I have not achieved it, but I focus on this one thing: Forgetting the past and looking forward to what lies ahead."

What values lies within you? Don't leave your gifts unopened. Don't ignore them. So, what do you like to do? What do you do best? Do you like to sing? Write? Arts and crafts? Do you enjoy cleaning? Do you have a love for children? Teaching? Helping others? Ask yourself: "When I was a child, what did I say I wanted to do when I grew up?"

No matter what you have a passion for, someone can always use what you have. What you have may just be what others need! Forget about your past mistakes. Forget about your fears. Forget about the opinions of others. Who you are depends on what you think about yourself, and moreso those things you believe about yourself.

Thoughts produce actions and actions produce results.

So, forget the lies of the past. Break every chain that keeps you bound. Run to win! Don't worry about how quickly you get to the finish line. Walk if you can, crawl if you must, fly if you will—just get there! Get to the other side of fear and rejection, comparison and competition.

Where Do I Go from Here?

Ignore the voices that tell you you're unworthy and say to you, "It can't be done." Remove the word "can't" from your vocabulary. No more with the "I don't have any money," or "I'm not educated," or "I'm too old," or "No one will help me" excuses. The list goes on and on. If you find yourself relating to this list, I employ you to arise with courage and faith! Press your way through to accomplish the tasks set before you. Let **NOTHING** stop you!

What has happened in the past will not direct my path today. I will no longer allow the negative words of others to dictate who I am or determine my results.

Patricia Hawthorne

YOU ARE TRANSFORMED

Romans 12:2 KJV

"And be not conformed to this world: but be ye transformed by the renewing of your mind, that ye may prove what is that good, and acceptable, and perfect will of God."

Where Do I Go from Here?

You are a new person. You are transformed. You are not to copy the fashions of the world, but to be wholly transfigured in accordance with God's will that He has chosen for you. When you are conformed to this world, you act as the world does. You act in opposition to undergo that total change which will bring you more in accordance with the will of God. You just have to change the way you think and develop new habits that produce new results.

Discover the purpose within you and offer it to someone else. Your purpose has always been there, just waiting for you to introduce it to the world.

For example, a chair is made to sit on, but it does not fulfill its purpose until it is made available for someone to actually sit on it.

As a child, I was shy and detached. I focused on good study habits. My head was often bowed down. I felt unworthy of what was handed to me, yet I had the favor of all my teachers, spiritual leaders, job, neighbors, and everyone I came into contact with. I truly believe I was surrounded by such caring people to help mold and shape me into the person I am today.

I fondly remember my first-grade teacher. She recognized something within me and spent time with me. She would sometimes take me home with her. She would also choose me to help her pass out papers or erase the blackboard. I see now that all of that was a preparation for my purpose to come forth.

When I entered junior high, I had a teacher who took time with me because she believed in me. She was the one who prepared me to be the Valedictorian in my junior year of high school. I didn't understand then what it was all about, but she would push me to do my homework when everyone else went to recess. She also pushed me to read many books and was always there for me.

When I was growing up in the church, the pastor's wife and the other leading ladies of the church took time with me. They, too, recognized my potential. They coached me, encouraged me, and gave me a gentle push when I was too afraid to progress. I began by speaking little poems on the Easter and Christmas holidays. Later, I did the welcome address for church programs and moved on to writing papers of encouragement in the church. In time, I moved into teaching and a leadership position of my own in the church.

After graduating high school, I went to New Orleans, Louisiana to find a job. I applied to South-Central Bell Telephone Company. At the time, they told me they couldn't hire me because of my slow typing speed. However, a month later they called me back and said they were going to take a chance on me. I was officially hired in 1972. While under their employ, they chose me to be their spokesperson for charitable donors. I was the one chosen to speak on behalf of the company about giving to nonprofits.

All throughout my life, I was being transformed into who I am today. My passion and purpose were enhanced and strengthened through school, church, and careers. Today, I am a Recording Artist, Writer, and Transformation Public Speaker. I speak words that are meant to transform and impact lives.

So, where do you go from here?

NOTES

Write what the scripture listed means to you on your journey to fulfilling YOUR purpose.

"And be not conformed to this world: but be ye transformed by the renewing of your mind, that ye may prove what is that good, and acceptable, and perfect will of God."
(Romans 12:2, KJV)

_____

_____

_____

_____

_____

_____

_____

_____

_____

_____

_____

_____

Where Do I Go from Here?

> HERE I AM, HERE I STAND
> WITH MY **PURPOSE** IN MY
> HAND; WITH A **PASSION**
> AND A DESIRE,
> WITH A HEART BURNING
> WITH FIRE,
> WITH IDEAS AND ENERGY
> I'M INSPIRED FOR VICTORY.

"You are the light of the world. A city on a hill cannot be hid."
~ Matthew 5:14 ~

STEP TWO

WHY ARE YOU HERE?

Patricia Hawthorne

PRAY

Philippians 4:6 NIV

"Do not be anxious about anything, but in every situation, by prayer and petition, with thanksgiving, present your requests to God."

Where Do I Go from Here?

Before you step into the purpose you were created for, always pray for direction. This is your roadmap to arrive safely to your destination. As you spend time talking and listening to God, He will show you what He wants to do in your life.

I recall being in church one night when the pastor was preaching about "purpose." That was the first time I really paid close attention to the word "purpose." He told us if we wanted to know our purpose, we should ask God to reveal it and to give us a scripture. So, we all closed our eyes and prayed for God to answer us.

I received my scripture as Acts chapter three. This scripture involves healing, preaching, and salvation. I also received a vision of a barrel filled with money. The barrel's supply of money was never-ending. Just as quickly as I would remove the money, the barrel would refill. That revelation came to me over 15 years ago.

Just recently, I discovered what my purpose was all about. While studying the Bible, the word "transformation" was revealed. I knew it was a divine word from the Lord. When I opened my business, I chose the butterfly as my logo and chose Romans 12:2 as my core passage: *"Be ye transformed by the renewing of your mind."*

"And this is the confidence that we have in Him, that if we ask for anything according to His will, He heareth us: and if we know that He hears us, whatsoever we ask, we know that we have the petitions that we desired of Him."
(1 John 5:14-15, KJV)

If you don't know your purpose yet, pray. Follow God's leading. In due time, I believe He will reveal it to you. You must understand that it's a step-by-step process of prayer and moving forward. Don't be worried or stressed out when things don't happen right away. Every purpose will go through its season.

Before you step into your purpose, it will take patience before you see it all come together. The journey will take lots of time. You will go through many trials, and you will make plenty of mistakes along the way. However, you must maintain a made-up mind, staying focused on the goal all the time. You must pray for direction and courage to stay the course.

CONSIDER YOUR PASSION

Psalms 37:4 KJV

"Delight yourself also in the LORD; and He shall give you the desires of your heart."

Passion is when you care deeply about something. Passion is a need to act; to do something or do something about. It's the excitement that moves you to respond. Passion creates energy. It empowers you to believe you can do "it." Passion energizes, motivates, and compels you to move forward.

What is your passion? What is that "thing" you love to do? What is it that you do better than anything else? What is it that gives you joy? How can you help someone else? What do they need that you have? How can you use what you have to help someone else? These insightful answers to these questions will lead you into your purpose.

When I was a child, I had a passion for writing inspirational poems and speeches. I kept all of my material neatly tucked away in a book. When I was in school, I entered a contest to speak for the Voice of Democracy. I won a savings bond for my college education.

In church, I was always chosen to speak or write papers of encouragement. As I got older, I discovered my gift was exhortation. That gift prompted me to open a greeting card business where I shared my poetry and speeches with others in cards.

I remember a friend asking me to make a card for her friend who was trying to decide whether or not to return to school. I was told that after her friend read my card, she was inspired and went back to school!

Today, I am sharing my inspiration with you in a book. My gifts of writing and speaking were a part of my life before I was born. Each step in life's journey has nourished my gifts and equipped me for my purpose.

What you are passionate about doing becomes your purpose.

First, identify what you're gifted at doing. What are others always complimenting you on?

Second, what is the need around you? Set out to help others.

Third, what do you enjoy doing? What excites you? List things you love to do in your free time.

Once you find your passion, you will begin to see your purpose. Take inventory of what gives you the greatest joy. For me, I experience my greatest joy when encouraging and motivating people to recognize who they really are and when they realize the gifts and talents within them as they realize the true reason they are here on Earth. I use my gifts of exhortation, teaching, and writing to benefit others.

There is a unique set of gifts, talents, skills, and abilities inside you that someone else needs in order to fulfill their life's purpose.

When I was growing up, I learned early on that I love to write poetry and inspirational papers. I also love to speak words of encouragement. I later discovered that everyone needs assistance at some point in time in their life. It was then I realized I have been fulfilling my purpose all my life without even knowing it!

I can recall when I was in school, I was always in the academics of competition. I enjoyed the debate, math, speaking, and spelling competitions. I also remember the favor that surrounded me as a child.

Where Do I Go from Here?

So, I ask you again: What is your passion? What do you have that others need? How can you help someone else? How do you find your purpose?

Patricia Hawthorne

DISCOVER YOUR PURPOSE

Jeremiah 29:11 GNT

"I alone know the plans I have for you, plans to bring you prosperity and not disaster; plans to bring about the future you hope for."

Where Do I Go from Here?

Purpose is the reason that something is created or exists. Knowing your purpose is knowing what God created you for. Discovering your purpose is a process that unfolds day by day.

What do people need from you? Are people changed from what you give them? Does their situation change?

Do you realize that people inspire people to change? Once you make a change, you make a difference. Passion and purpose work together. They help to unlock your potential. Passion may drive you, but purpose will pull you. Purpose inspires you, gives you energy, and plants ideas. This journey is filled with hard lessons along the way. Make no mistake about it; you have a purpose to express both effectively and powerfully. You have been chosen for a specific mission for such a time as this. Your purpose holds your gifts, passions, and values. Look inward and see yourself. Look outward and see your purpose. The world is waiting for you!

To discover your purpose, know that it is a day-by-day process. Anything that is not a part of your purpose is a distraction. When you discover your purpose, your actions and decisions will get in line with your purpose. Your career, friends, and what you allow to influence you will all line up in agreement. Go ahead and step into your purpose!

After retiring from South Central Bell, I was inspired by my pastor to open my own business. I called it "Making a Difference." I decided to put words of encouragement inside greeting cards. I obtained my business license when I had no product. I had help to design the cards, and I would write an encouraging poem for each card. Then, I started making customized cards. I remember a lady who wanted me to make a custom card to encourage and help her friend. The report came back that her friend was, indeed, encouraged to go back to school (that was the purpose of the card). The joy I experienced inspired and encouraged me to continue!

At the age of 66, my daughter inspired me to go back to college to obtain my Bachelor's Degree in Communication. In 2015, I graduated from the University of Texas of the Premium Basin in Odessa, Texas.

Where Do I Go from Here?

After graduating, I then changed my business name from "Making a Difference" to "People Inspiring Change."

Later, I wrote a poem all about purpose. I then took that poem and began to sing the words. From that poem, I wrote six songs and in 2017, released a CD titled *Moving Forward*. That was when I truly discovered my true purpose and a burning desire to help others see their purpose. I began to move forward to share it with the world.

So, where do you go from here?

NOTES

Write what the scripture listed means to you on your journey to fulfilling YOUR purpose.

"I alone know the plans I have for you, plans to bring you prosperity and not disaster, plans to bring about the future you hope for."
(Jeremiah 29:11, GNT)

_____

_____

_____

_____

_____

_____

_____

_____

_____

_____

_____

_____

_____

_____

Where Do I Go from Here?

> I'M MOVING FORWARD DAY BY DAY, WITH PERSISTENCE LEADING MY WAY. I'M MOVING FORWARD WITH A MADE-UP MIND, STAYIN FOCUSED ALL THE TIME. IF I FALL…IF I FAIL, I SHALL RISE TO PREVAIL.
>
> NO MATTER WHAT PEOPLE MAY SAY, I SEE THE VISION FROM FAR AWAY. NO MATTER WHAT COMES AGAINST ME, I HAVE A DATE WITH DESTINY.

"Where there is no vision, the people perish."
~ Proverbs 29:18 ~

Where Do I Go from Here?

STEP THREE
MOVE FORWARD

Patricia Hawthorne

SEE THE VISION

Habakkuk 2:2-3 KJV

"And the LORD answered me, and said, 'Write the vision, and make it plain upon tables, so he may run that reads it. For the vision is yet for an appointed time, but at the end it shall speak, and not lie: though it tarry, wait for it; because it will surely come, it will not tarry.'"

Where Do I Go from Here?

Get a clear picture in your mind of your vision. Stay focused on your vision. Let it inspire and motivate you to keep moving forward.

Vision is the strategy behind fulfilling your purpose. It will elevate your mind to the truth that yes, there are more possibilities for you. It reveals that there is more than what you see around you or more than what you are being told. Your vision has the power to change everything.

Vision reminds you of the cause to move. It is a powerful force to make you move in pursuit of things bigger than you.

As mentioned previously, you have unlimited power living inside of you, but you have not yet tapped into it. That greatness and power residing in you are just waiting to be fulfilled, and that can happen when you apply the gifts and talents God gave you.

Focus on your vision and make those dreams a reality!

While in college, more and more of my purpose was revealed in visions. So, I created a vision collage. A vision collage is precisely what it sounds like: a vision for one's life. While making my collage, I was very specific in choosing images that appealed to me without even knowing why. My collage looked something like this:

In creating the collage, the vision of the barrel of money never running out came to my remembrance. While in college, I developed the idea of training businesses on great customer service. I began to see myself as a college graduate, professional public inspirational speaker, and writer. The new CD, "Moving

Forward," was not a part of my collage, but it did end up being a part of my book.

Let me be an example for you. Today, I am an Inspiration and Transformation Speaker, Recording Artist, and Life-Changing Writer! I feel this is my vision, purpose, and most of all, my destiny!

Patricia Hawthorne

PURSUE YOUR PURPOSE

Proverbs 18:16 ESV

"A gift opens the way and ushers the giver into the presence of the great."

Where Do I Go from Here?

You are here for a reason. You are here for a season. You were created for a purpose. You are filled with gifts and talents that can inspire someone else. Everything you need to move forward and fulfill your purpose is already within you. You were born with a purpose. I get joy from using my gifts of writing and speaking and using my exhortation to empower others to pursue their purpose and fulfill their destiny. Purpose makes like meaningful.

When you make people happy, you are happy, too! Take small steps. Be patient, continue to persist, and move forward. It will take you on a journey to build your character, confidence, and faith.

Now that I understand I have a purpose, I can move forward to fulfill it and reach my full potential in life. I am in hot pursuit of what belongs to me. I can now see that the trials and tribulations I have endured and the failures and mistakes I have made did not come to destroy me, but rather to propel me into my destiny.

Don't allow fear to hinder you. The next time you are tempted to quit pursuing your purpose because of fear, think of those who need and are depending on you to share your gifts, talents, skills, and abilities so that they can fulfill their individual purpose. Get excited and fired up about your dreams and purpose! Be willing to make mistakes. Be prepared to fail. Be content with defeat. Why? Every purpose is a journey. It's a process. It has its season of growth. There is a new adventure to be had every single day. Your purpose is an eternal pursuit. Pursue your purpose with Godlike power and energy. God is always working in and through you.

I am often encouraged to complete my mission when I hear of children with disabilities fulfilling their God-given purpose. My faith moves up another level. I have seen many of these children running marathons, playing sports, graduating from college, delivering wonderful speeches, dedicated to helping others, and even having a desire to be the President of the United States! How awesome is that? Although they have more challenges than I, they move forward as though nothing can stop them.

So, I ask you: What is YOUR excuse?

Where Do I Go from Here?

Discover your awesome purpose and start walking by faith, not by sight. Faith is the substance of things you hope for and the evidence of what you don't see. If you can believe it, you can receive it. If you have that burning desire, you can achieve it. Believe that things are going to work out for you!

Patricia Hawthorne

BE PERSISTENT

1 Corinthians 15:58 NIV

"Therefore, my dear brothers and sisters, stand firm. Let nothing move you. Always give yourselves fully to the work of the Lord, because you know that your labor in the Lord is not in vain."

Where Do I Go from Here?

This journey takes persistence in spite of opposition, obstacles, discouragement, etc. You must persevere. You must endure. You must continue.

Press toward the goal, as one who is running a race. The prize can be yours — if you do not faint, tire, or look back. As you begin to move forward and step into your purpose, you will need the persistence to get the job done! Allow God to lead, guide, and strengthen you. Stay persistent and endure to the end.

I went to college for five years at the age of 66. I believe this was my greatest challenge in life. I was working while going to school. Many of you know about studying for test after test. Sometimes, I studied until 5:00 a.m., rested briefly, and was back at it for work at 8:00 a.m.

When I look back, it didn't seem possible to make A's and B's — let alone graduate. However, I stayed focused on my goal to finish with excellent grades. I ran out of funding and had to stay out a semester and transfer to another college. In 2015, both my daughter and I graduated! I remember going to her graduation and there was a young lady who told her inspiring story. She had tried to commit suicide, but her teachers and counselors cared enough to help her make it through. She told us how she had to persevere through all the obstacles in her way. I thought, "If she can do it, so can I!"

When I returned to school, I had a renewed mind. I gained a new determination. That young lady ignited a fire within me, and nothing could stop me from reaching my goal. We never know how our story will impact the lives of others.

Let nothing stop you. Be patient. Stay focused all the time. Move forward day by day with persistence leading your way. No matter what people may say, you see the vision from far away. Keep pressing on. Your goal is near. Don't procrastinate. Don't fear.

Where Do I Go from Here?

NOTES

Write what the scripture listed means to you on your journey to fulfilling YOUR purpose.

"And the LORD answered me, and said, 'Write the vision, and make it plain upon tables, so he may run that reads it. For the vision is yet for an appointed time, but at the end it shall speak, and not lie: though it tarry, wait for it; because it will surely come, it will not tarry."
(Habakkuk 2:2, KJV)

_____

_____

_____

_____

_____

_____

_____

_____

_____

_____

_____

_____

_____

Patricia Hawthorne

Where Do I Go from Here?

> *I'M PRESSING ON.*
> *MY GOAL IS NEAR.*
> *I WON'T PROCRASTINATE;*
> *I WON'T FEAR.*
> *IF THERE'S A WILL,*
> *THERE'S A WAY.*
> *I'M ON COURSE*
> *AND I WON'T STRAY.*
> *I'M **DEDICATED**.*
> *I WON'T GIVE IN.*
> *I'M **DETERMINED***
> *TO REACH THE END.*

"Stand firm. Let nothing move you."
~ 1 Corinthians 15:58 ~

STEP FOUR

NEVER GIVE UP

Patricia Hawthorne

NEVER GIVE UP

Galatians 6:9 NIV

"Let us not become weary in doing good, for at the proper time, we will reap a harvest if we do not give up."

FIRST: BE PATIENT

Before you step into your purpose, you will need patience. Keep in mind, there is always a reason and a season for everything.

You need the patience to remain calm when dealing with difficult situations, tasks, or people. You need the patience to endure trials, patience to move in your season, and patience in waiting for clear direction to know where to go from here. Even in this microwave generation, you must realize that these things take time. Don't be in a rush. Don't worry about anything. Continue to move in the direction of your vision and dream. Be confident that God will bring it all to pass. Believe in yourself and continue to move forward. Never give up!

Not only do you have a purpose; there is a season for your purpose to be offered to the world. There is a season for everything under the sun. Throughout life, you are being prepared, trained, and equipped to serve others with your purpose. It may take you longer than others — and that's okay! Your purpose can be delayed because the timing isn't right. Sometimes, your purpose is delayed because of fear, procrastination, or others' opinions of you. Other times, you may make poor choices. Nevertheless, your purpose will surely show up. It is up to you to recognize it, nourish it, and move forward with it. Whatever you do, don't give up on the process!

SECOND: BE CONSISTENT

Be consistent! Persevere! Press! Endure until the end!

Complete assignments given to you. Some tasks will be harder than others. Remember always that *"all things are possible with God"* (Mark 10:27, NIV) and *"I can do all this through Him who gives me strength"* (Philippians 4:13, NIV).

I remember hearing about a lady who did nothing but meet the soldiers with a hug when they returned home. You may ask yourself, "What's so important about a hug?" Well, this particular woman was always there to show them love and appreciation for keeping our country safe.

For some reason, I have never forgotten her story. I was so inspired by her compassion, my own purpose became much clearer. Now, I want to empower others to find their God-given purpose. I began to think of the homeless, the prisoners, our youth…the list can go on and on. Talking about making a difference? That lady is a perfect example! She ignited the fire that was already within me.

While stepping into your purpose, keep moving forward—no matter what happens. Be firm and steadfast. Have a made-up mind and stay focused all the time. Stay on course. Be watchful for distractions and roadblocks on your journey.

THIRD: BE DETERMINED

Decide to achieve your goal. Let your decision be settled, resolute, and unwavering. Don't allow others' opinions to influence your decisions. Remain positive with the expectation that you will win.

Where there is a will, there is a way. Stay on course and don't stray. Be dedicated; don't give in. Be determined to reach the end. If you fall…if you fail, rise up and prevail. You have been called for such a time as this. Trust God to guide you to do what He wants to do through you. Never give up!

You are a gift to the world. Don't leave your gift unopened. Start today! Tap into your passion and desires. Tap into the burning fire within you! The graveyard is filled with dead purposes—people who never completed their assignment for which they were created. They never discovered the real reason they were chosen to be here on Earth. What a shame!

NOTES

Write what the scripture listed means to you on your journey to fulfilling YOUR purpose.

"Therefore, my dear brothers and sisters, stand firm. Let nothing move you. Always give yourselves fully to the work of the Lord, because you know that your labor in the Lord is not in vain."
(1 Corinthians 15:58, NIV)

_____

_____

_____

_____

_____

_____

_____

_____

_____

_____

_____

_____

_____

Where Do I Go from Here?

CONCLUSION

As you begin to move forward, be steadfast and unmovable. Stay focused on your goals. No matter what comes your way, don't fear, don't procrastinate, and don't give in. Be determined to reach the end. Most importantly, learn from every step you take in life's journey. If you fall…if you fail, rise up and prevail. Your trials are only for a moment, but your joy comes in the morning. When is morning? Morning is when you wake up to pursue the purpose within you.

Wake up, everyone!

Have a Wonderful and Prosperous day!

LIFE-CHANGING STEPS MADE SIMPLE

1. Know who you are.
2. Know why you are here.
3. Don't be afraid to move forward.
4. Never give up.

Patricia Hawthorne

DECLARE TODAY:

I am transformed.

I am brand new.

I am somebody.

I have a new attitude!

I remove "can't" from my vocabulary.

I refuse to be discouraged; rather, I encourage myself.

I refuse to give up.

I am worthy of my calling and purpose.

I want to do all I'm called to do.

No matter what comes against me, I am destined for victory.

I shall pursue my goals.

If I fall…if I fail…I shall rise to prevail!

Speak it! Believe it! See it!

ABOUT THE AUTHOR

Patricia Hawthorne is an Inspiration and Transformation Speaker, Recording Artist, and Life-Changing Writer. She feels this is her vision, her purpose, and most of all, her destiny! Patricia received her B.A. in Communications in 2015 from UTPB at the age of 66. In 2017, she released her first CD titled *Moving Forward*. In 2019, she published this book, *Where Do I Go from Here?* Patricia is the proud Owner of "People Inspiring Change," which is impacting and transforming lives.

Patricia loves to share words of encouragement and strength with others. She desires to make a positive impact in the lives of others. She is committed to producing change by inspiring people to recognize their purpose and empowering them to reach their full potential. She provides strategies and resources others need to achieve their goals effectively and efficiently.

In 1994, Patricia was inspired by her pastor to start a greeting card business that she called "Making A Difference." Her store carried inspirational customized cards and gifts that ministered words of love, courage, strength, and hope. In 1996, she also studied Biblical Counseling from Friends International Bible College. She was also a spokeswoman for major charities while working for Lucent Technologies in New Orleans, Louisiana, from which she retired in 1999.

In 2005, Patricia relocated to Taylor, Texas due to Hurricane Katrina. She recently changed the name of her company from "Making A Difference" to "People Inspiring Change." She began moving forward to release the seed of greatness within her to fulfill her passion.

Where Do I Go from Here?

CONTACT PATRICIA

You are invited to visit her **website** at:
www.peopleinspiringchange.com

Email:
phawthorne@peopleinspiringchange.com

Phone:
504.812.5688

Patricia Hawthorne

www.ingramcontent.com/pod-product-compliance
Lightning Source LLC
Chambersburg PA
CBHW052206110526
44591CB00012B/2094